AF374816

HAPPY HATS HOLIDAY HOOEY

BY CALIEB BARNES

ILLUSTRATED BY DAVID SCHIMMEL

BX PUBLISHING

ISBN: 979-8-9914665-1-6 (Hardcover)
ISBN: 979-8-2185706-2-0 (E-Book)

Library of Congress Control Number: 2024926071

Any references to historical events, real people, or real places are used fictitiously. Names, characters, and places are products of the author's imagination.

Author Calieb Barnes
Illustration by David Schimmel

Printed in the United States of America.

First printing Edition 2024.

BxPublishing, LLC.

3195 Dayton-Xenia Rd.
STE 900 #180
Beavercreek, OH 45434-6391

BxPublishingllc@gmail.com
www.BxPublishing .com

Dedicated to:

The Toscano's

There is so much I've always wanted
to say. But I could never find the words.
Even now, there is no simple way to express the
immensity of both my sorrow and my appreciation
simultaneously.
Just know that you are truly loved and treasured.

Happy Holidays

~Calieb

I MAY LOOK LIKE A HAT,
BUT I'M MUCH MORE THAN THAT
IN FACT I'LL BE YOUR GUIDE.

THE BELLS AND THE HOLLY
EVERYONE'S JOLLY
AGAIN COMES THE YULE TIDE

MAKE SURE YOU DON'T WAIT
SHOULD YOU DECORATE,
UNTANGLE AND STRING UP THE LIGHTS

THE WINDOW TRIMMERS
WILL TWINKLE AND SHIMMER
AGLOW, IT'S QUITE A SITE

Douglas
Fir
Sitka
Spruce
Blue
Spruce

Sitka Spruce
YOU'LL NEXT NEED A TREE,
AND SHOULD YOU ASK ME
I'D PICK A BIG BLUE SPRUCE

Blue Spruce
Nothing quite like a Blue Spruce
DESPITE IT'S ODD NAME,
IT'S GREEN ALL THE SAME
A FAVORITE OF MOOSE AND SNOW GOOSE

Nice One !

WHAT WILL SANTA BRING
WHILE THE CAROLERS SING
WE MUST ALL JUST WAIT AND SEE.

A SHINY NEW BIKE,
A DOLLHOUSE IF YOU LIKE
THEY BOTH COULD BE UNDER THE TREE

WAY UP ON THE ICE
THERE'S THE "NAUGHTY OR NICE",
IT'S A LIST ROLLED LIKE A SCROLL

Naugh

SO MAKE SURE TO THINK TWICE
AND BE EXTRA NICE
FOR THE NAUGHTY GET ONLY COAL
NICE
COAL

Santa's
Workshop

North
pole
AT SANTA'S WORKSHOP,
WAY UP ON TOP,
SITS A PLACE CALLED THE NORTH POLE

THE TOYS ARE TOP-SHELF,
HAND MADE BY THE ELF
EVERY TOY IT'S OWN CUBBYHOLE

Sante Fe Express
Yahtzee
Mouse Trap
Operation
Board Games
Toy Trains
WAR DOG
VOLTRON
Dolls
Video Games
THEN COMES SAINT NICK
AND THE TOYS HE HAS PICKED,
FOR IT'S BETTER TO GIVE THAN RECEIVE

BUT HE'S NOT JUST THE GIVER,
HE WILL PERSONALLY DELIVER
TO ALL ON CHRISTMAS EVE.

AND THERE IS ONLY ONE WAY
TO REACH ALL IN ONE DAY
IT IS RUDOLPH AND HIS SHINY RED NOSE

HO-HO-HO
FOR ALL STOP AND STARE
AS THEY FLY THROUGH THE AIR
SANTA LAUGHING HIS DEEP HO-HO-HO'S

WITH RED COAT AND HAT
SO JOLLY TO LOOK AT,
HIS FEET IN BLACK SHINY BOOTS

WHITE GLOVES ON HIS KNUCKLES,
BLACK BELT WITH GOLD BUCKLES,
DOWN YOUR CHIMNEY HE WILL SOON SHOOT

SO TRY TO SLEEP TIGHT
COME CHRISTMAS EVE NIGHT
FOR MORNING CAN'T COME FAST ENOUGH

21:00

Tommy
John

AND ONCE THE DAY BREAKS
AND EVERYONE WAKES,
YOU'LL FIND YOUR STOCKINGS BEEN STUFFED

AND NO MATTER THE WEATHER
FAMILIES GATHER TOGETHER
TO WALK DOWN MEMORY LANE

THE SEASONAL TREATS
SWEET CANDIES TO EAT
STRINGED POPCORN AND STRIPED CANDY CANES

THE WONDERS AND JOYS,
THE GIFTS AND THE TOYS,
SO MAGICAL IN EVERY WAY.

THROUGH CHRISTMAS TIMES
THE SONGS AND RHYMES
CELEBRATE THE HOLIDAY!

www.ingramcontent.com/pod-product-compliance
Lightning Source LLC
Chambersburg PA
CBRC090943120726
48010CB00012B/329